D1175743

Yellow Umbrella Books are published by Capstone Press
151 Good Counsel Drive, P.O. Box 669, Mankato, Minnesota 56002
http://www.capstone-press.com

Library of Congress Cataloging-in-Publication Data
Curry, Don L.
    Stars/by Don L. Curry.
    p. cm.
    Includes index.
    ISBN 0-7368-0726-8
    1. Stars—Juvenile literature. [1. Stars.] I. Title.
QB801.7 .C87   2001
523.8—dc21   00-033013

    Summary: Describes what stars are and various types of stars, including the sun and
several constellations.

Editorial Credits:
Susan Evento, Managing Editor/Product Development; Elizabeth Jaffe, Senior Editor;
    Dawn Harrison, Designer; Kimberly Danger and Heidi Schoof, Photo Researchers

Photo Credits:
Cover: David Nunuk/Westlight; Title Page: Bill & Sally Fletcher (top left), Unicorn Stock
Photos/Jeff Greenberg (bottom left), Corbis/Craig Aurness (top right), Bill & Sally Fletcher
(bottom right); Page 2 & 3: Bill & Sally Fletcher; Page 4: Bill & Sally Fletcher; Page 6:
Corbis/Bill Ross; Page 7: Unicorn Stock Photos/Jeff Greenberg; Page 8: Corbis/R. Watts; Page
10 & 11: Bill & Sally Fletcher; Page 12: Richard Norton/Science Graphics (top and bottom);
Page 13: Bill & Sally Fletcher; Page 14: Bill & Sally Fletcher; Page 15: Corbis/Craig Aurness;
Page 16: Richard Hamilton Smith

Art on pages 4, 5, and 9 by Shelley Dieterichs.

1 2 3 4 5 6 06 05 04 03 02 01

10/04

STARS

BY DON L. CURRY

Consulting Editor: Gail Saunders-Smith, Ph.D.
Consultants: Claudine Jellison and Patricia Williams
Reading Recovery Teachers
Content Consultant: Gregory Vogt, NASA

Yellow Umbrella Books

an imprint of Capstone Press
Mankato, Minnesota

Have you ever looked up
at a clear night sky?

You see so many stars that you cannot count all of them.

A star is a big, hot ball of gas that spins in space.

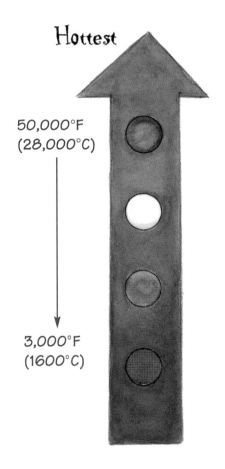

Hottest

50,000°F
(28,000°C)

3,000°F
(1600°C)

How hot is a star? You can tell how hot a star is by its color.

A blue star is the hottest.

A white star is really hot.

A yellow star is hot.

A red star is the coolest star.

Can you name a star?

The Sun is a star.
The Sun is a yellow star
that we can see
in the daytime.
It gives us light
and keeps us warm.

How big is the Sun?
A million Earths would fit
inside the Sun!
The Sun might look like
it is the biggest star,
but it is not.
It is the closest star to Earth,
so it looks the biggest.

Stars come in all sizes.
The Sun is a medium-sized star,
called a dwarf star.
Some stars are smaller
than the Sun.
Some stars, called giant stars,
are much bigger than the Sun.

A constellation is a group of stars that make up a picture. This constellation is named the Big Dipper.

Look to see if you can find
the dipper.
A dipper is a cup
with a long handle.

Now try to find the Little Dipper.

Can you find the Big Dog?

The Big Dog's head is
shaped like a triangle.
The star in the Big Dog's neck
is called Sirius.
It is the second brightest star.

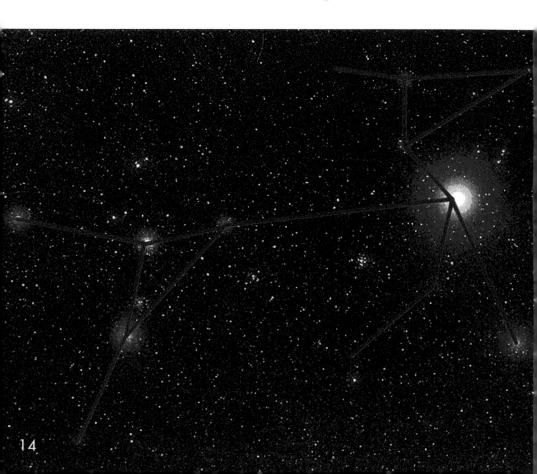

Where are stars
during the day?
The stars are still around us.
But the Sun's bright light keeps
us from seeing them.

At night, Earth blocks
the Sun's light.
Then we can see
the many stars
that light up the sky.

Words to Know/Index

Big Dipper—a group of stars in the night sky that looks like a large spoon; page 10

blue star—the hottest type of star; page 5

constellation—a group of stars in the night sky, usually named after something that it looks like; page 10

dwarf star—a star that is average in size; page 9

Earth—the planet on which we live; pages 8, 16

giant—very large; page 9

Little Dipper—a group of stars in the night sky that looks like a small spoon; page 12

medium—average or middle; page 9

million—a thousand thousands (1,000,000); page 8

red star—the coolest type of star; page 5

Sirius—the name of a very bright star, also called the Dog Star; page 14

white star—a star that is very, very hot, but not as hot as the hottest stars; page 5

yellow star—a star that is very hot, like the Sun; pages 5, 7

Word Count: 295
Early-Intervention Levels: 13–16